School of the Blues Less
Blues Keyboard M
Level 2
by
Steve Czarnecki and Dave Barrett

GW00373018

CD Contents

1	Examples 1.1 to 1.5 [1:29]	24	Example 2.19 [0:30]
2	Examples 1.6 to 1.11 [1:23]	25	Examples 2.20 to 2.25 [1:57]
3	Examples 1.12 to 1.19 [1:37]	26	"Steve's Blues" Study Song [2:38]
4	Examples 1.20 to 1.28 [3:33]	27	"Mike's Revenge" Study Song [3:27]
5	Examples 1.29 to 1.32 [2:23]	28	Example 4.1 to 4.2 [0:25]
6	Example 2.1 [0:39]	29	Example 4.3 [0:34]
7	Example 2.2 [0:43]	30	Examples 4.4 to 4.10 [1:24]
8	Example 2.3 [0:26]	31	Examples 4.11 to 4.15 [1:25]
9	Example 2.4 [0:28]	32	Examples 4.16 to 4.20 [1:42]
10	Example 2.5 [0:15]	33	Example 4.21 [0:34]
11	Example 2.6 [0:28]	34	Example 4.22 [0:33]
12	Example 2.7 [0:36]	35	Example 4.23 [0:39]
13	Example 2.8 [0:46]	36	Example 4.24 [0:34]
14	Example 2.9 [0:41]	37	Example 4.25 [0:33]
15	Example 2.10 [0:45]	38	Example 5.1 [0:36]
16	Example 2.11 [0:35]	39	Example 5.2 [0:21]
17	Example 2.12 [0:39]	40	Example 5.3 [0:20]
18	Example 2.13 [0:45]	41	Example 5.4 [0:21]
19	Example 2.14 [0:31]	42	Example 5.5 [0:23]
20	Example 2.15 [0:32]	43	Example 5.6 [0:24]
21	Example 2.16 [0:30]	44	Example 5.7 [0:24]
22	Example 2.17 [0:31]	45	Example 5.8 [0:43]
23	Example 2.18 [0:33]		

1 2 3 4 5 6 7 8 9 0

Visit us on the Web at www.melbay.com — E-mail us at email@melbay.com

Table of Contents

About This Method

This book in the *School of the Blues Lesson Series* is aimed toward the intermediate pianist interested in learning to play the Blues. This book continues where the first book, *Blues Keyboard Method, Level 1 (MB21060BCD)*, left off and is organized in the following way:

In Chapter 1 we'll continue our understanding of chord structure by adding notes to our basic three-note chord (triad). We'll also take a look at playing in Minor.

In Chapter 2 we'll work on developing your accompaniment skills. Sometimes you'll be playing by yourself (self accompaniment) and other times you'll be a supportive member of a band. In this chapter we'll dig into the common ways that you'll approach these different situations.

In Chapter 3 I've written some songs for you to study. This will not only challenge you to bring your keyboard skills to the next step, but it will also give you broader valuable lick-vocabulary (not to mention that it's fun to learn and play full songs).

In Chapter 4 I'm going to present some basic musical material you can use in your right hand—either in a band situation or when playing solo. We'll also discuss the role of the left hand in Blues piano.

Finally, in Chapter 5, we'll focus expressly on the study of Blues for the organ.

Thanks To

I'd like to thank David Barre and the folks at School of the Blues for the opportunity to share my music with a wider audience through these books. Also thanks to my wife Jeanne and my daughter Sara for their inspiration and support and in particular to Sara for her complete command of the written word.

I would also like to thank the following people for their contribution to this book and recording.

- Producer, Editor & Co-author – David Barrett
- Proof Readers – Sara Czarnecki, Dennis Carelli & Diane Smith
- Photography – Dave Lepori Photography in San Jose, California

About the Author

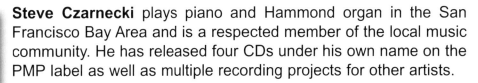

Steve Czarnecki plays piano and Hammond organ in the San Francisco Bay Area and is a respected member of the local music community. He has released four CDs under his own name on the PMP label as well as multiple recording projects for other artists.

When I Dream of You and *Sunnyside Up* showcase Steve's Jazz piano skills. The *Soul/Jazz Quintet* features Steve's Hammond organ chops along with vocalist Nate Pruitt, also a teacher at School of the Blues. *Soul Rendezvous* is his latest CD and features Steve's original compositions.

Steve has worked and played with many musicians in his career including Robben Ford, Mark Ford, Ernie Watts, Alphonse Mouzon, Barney Kessel, Kenny Rankin, John Garcia, Charlie Musselwhite and others. His current group, Steve Czarnecki's Soul/Jazz Quintet, performs in the San Francisco Bay Area. He's also a f the Blues All-Star Band. He can be found at his website www.soul-jazz.com.

t the School of the Blues Lesson Series

School of the Blues is a school dedicated to the study of Blues and all the styles it influenced. Founded in 2002 by educator David Barrett, the school thrives today as the center of Blues education in the San Jose/San Francisco, California Bay Area.

The instructors at the School of the Blues have on average about twenty years of experience in performance and teaching, and were hand-picked by the school for both their playing and teaching skills, knowledge of their instrument, and ability to teach at all levels of group and private instruction. They are incredibly dedicated to their craft, and enjoy being a part of their students' musical and personal development as well-rounded musicians.

They are also the co-authors of these lesson series, along with David Barrett who is co-author and administrator to all the School of the Blues books.

These books have been crafted with meticulous attention by the authors, making sure that their experience and knowledge is reflected in each lesson, all with the goal of continuing the education of the Blues to all who are interested.

As this series is designed for students of other instruments to play together, we encourage you to tell other aspiring musicians about this series so you can all learn together. Music is meant to be shared

We all wish you the best of luck in your studies. For more information about this series, or to contact us, please visit www.SchoolOfTheBlues.com.

Chapter 1 – Understanding More Music Theory

In *Blues Keyboard Method, Level 1* (MB21060BCD) we introduced the idea that chords, groups of three or more notes played simultaneously, are derived from scales. If you'll recall, we took the C Major scale (Ex. 1.1) and added two notes above each note in the scale. These two notes were in thirds on the same scale (Ex. 1.2). We call these groupings triads, referring to the fact that they contain three notes. They are three note chords.

Ex. 1.1

Ex. 1.2

We then extended these chords by one note (Ex. 1.3). We added one note to each chord a third above the highest note. This gave us a set of four note chords. We made much of the fact that the Dominant 7th chord (G7 in the key of C) was an indispensable element in Blues music. Now we're going to examine some of the other chords and see how they're used.

Ex. 1.3

Let's look at the chord built on C (Ex. 1.4). It contains the C Major triad with the Major 7th added (the distance between the root C and the 7th, B, is a Major 7th). This chord is called a C Major 7th chord. Note the fact that the word Major in its name refers to the fact that it's a Major triad with its seventh added.

Ex. 1.4

Now, let's examine the second chord in our series (Ex. 1.5). This is called a D Minor 7th chord. It's our original D Minor triad with its 7th (which happens to be a Minor 7th) added. You'll notice that the Minor in the name refers to the "Minor-ness" of the chord (that is its Minor third) and not the coincidence of its Minor 7th.

Ex. 1.5

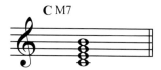

Next, let's look at the 7th chord built on the 5th degree of the scale: G7 (Ex 1.6). We discussed in the first book the vital importance of this Dominant 7th chord in the Blues. As we revisit it, we're again struck by two facts: 1. This is the only chord made up of a Major triad with a Minor 7th added, and 2. This is the only dominant seventh chord in the key of C.

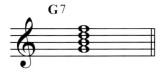

Now that we've extended these chords up to a seventh, why can't we build them out further? In Example 1.7 we take the C Major chord to its full extension. As we add notes a third above the previous notes we get successively the 9th, 11th and 13th.

Ex. 1.7

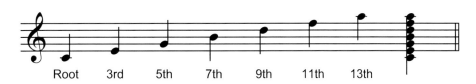

Shall we continue? What if we add one more above the thirteenth (Ex. 1.8)? Is this a Fifteenth? No, sorry, that's a trick question. The C is the root regardless of its position in the chord. The known universe of the C chord, or any triadic chord for that matter, is 1—3—5—7—9—11—13.

Ex. 1.8

If I play the following chord, what do I have?

Ex. 1.9

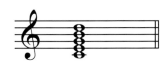

C Major 9th is correct. We usually name the chord according to the quality of the foundation triad (Major, Minor, Diminished or Augmented) and its highest upper voice (7, 9, 11, and 13). Let's apply these rules to our Minor chords. Here is the D Minor chord built out to its fullest. Since the highest upper voice is the B (the 13th). This chord is a Dm13.

Ex. 1.10

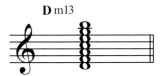

Going to our Dominant 7th (G7) we'll apply the same procedure. Example 1.11 is a G13. Note the absence of the word Major or Minor indicates that this is a Dominant 7th chord, and not a Major or Minor chord.

Ex. 1.11

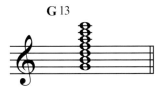

These upper voices (9, 11 and 13) basically add coloration to the chord. They do not change a Major to a Minor or a Minor to a Dominant 7th. They give you a richer, more interesting Major, Minor or Dominant 7th chord. In certain styles of music (Jazz or sophisticated Blues) they are highly prized. In more rudimentary Blues styles they would not be appropriate.

You may notice that in the Major and Dominant 13th chords, the 11th (C) seems to clash with the rest of the chord because of the dissonance created with the third (B). Therefore, we will usually leave the 11th out when we play a G13 for example (Ex. 1.12) or a C Major 13th (Ex. 1.13).

Ex. 1.12

Ex. 1.13

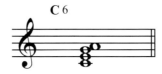

A further note on terminology: The C Major chord with the 13th added (Ex. 1.14) will sometimes be called a C Major 6 or C6 chord (the 13th is the 6th scale degree). Similarly, a Gm13 chord may be called a Gm6. This is common practice even though it flies in the face of theory.

Ex. 1.14

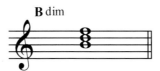

You may notice that I've left one chord out of our study: the chord built on the 7th degree of the scale. It is a diminished triad. To diminish means to make smaller, and as you can see (Ex 1.15), this chord contains a Minor third and a Diminished 5th. Both the intervals are smaller than the major 3rd and Perfect 5th in a Major chord.

Ex. 1.15

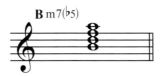

If we add the 7th to this chord (Ex. 1.16) we have what is known as a B Half-Diminished 7th chord, or sometimes a Bm7♭5. A true B diminished chord would be a series of Minor thirds, but you'll notice here the interval between the root and the 7th is actually a Minor 7th. The Bm7♭5 nomenclature refers to the fact that if we raised the F Natural to an F♯, we'd be looking at a Bm7 chord.

Ex. 1.16

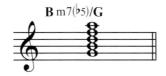

The B Half-Diminished can be extended out like all the other chords (Ex. 1.17).

Ex. 1.17

By the way, if you were to add a G below the B Half-Diminished, you'd get a G9 chord (Ex. 18).

Ex. 1.18

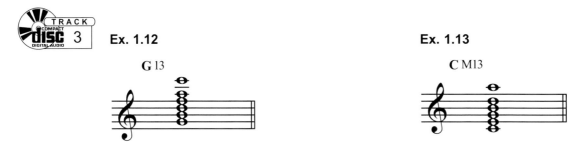

In fact, the B Half-Diminished acts in a similar fashion to the G7 chord with which it shares many notes (that is, it wants to resolve to C Major). This is demonstrated below.

Ex. 1.19

As you'll recall from book one, we can create a harmonization for any melody in the key of C Major with these chords derived from the key of C Major. Of course there are times when a song doesn't start on a Major chord, but a Minor chord, and may even end on a Minor chord. Therefore we'll spend a little time on the subject of Minor keys.

Minor Keys

Below is the *A Natural* or *Pure Minor* scale (Ex. 1.20). As you can see, it's nothing more than the C Major scale played from A to A. Even though the notes are the same, their relative level of importance differs. In C Major, you'd expect a melody to start on a C and certainly end on a C. All other notes would be defined in their relation to C. C would be the most important note. Now, in A Minor, A will be the prime note. A melody in A Minor may start on A and will most likely end on A (Ex. 1.21).

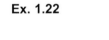

Ex. 1.20

Ex. 1.21

The chord built on G will no longer be the second to last chord in the song leading conclusively to C. In this case (A Minor) it will be the chord built on E that leads to the final chord. Here is an A Minor scale with all its chords in triadic form (Ex 1.22).

Ex. 1.22

If you create a random progression, starting on A Minor and eventually ending there (Ex. 1.23), you'll notice the overall darkness of the Minor key. It definitely has a more somber tone than that of our previous Major examples.

Ex. 1.23

Now, look at the following Minor key progression. What have we here? Again we hear the Minor tonality, but the chord before the final A Minor is an E Major. That G♯ isn't even in the A natural Minor scale. What's happening?

Ex. 1.24

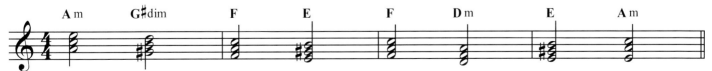

Interestingly enough, Minor keys are less defined than Major scales in the sixth and seventh degrees of the scale. In fact one scale, the Melodic Minor, has notes that differ in its ascending and descending versions. Let's take a look at the following Harmonic Minor (Ex. 1.25) and Melodic Minor (Ex. 1.26) scales.

Ex. 1.25 – A Harmonic Minor

Ex. 1.26 – A Melodic Minor

Whereas in the Major keys you only have one set of notes that make up the scale, in Minor keys, the 6th can be natural (as in the Natural, Harmonic and descending versions of the Melodic Minor scales) or sharped (as in the ascending version of the Melodic Minor scale) and the seventh may be natural (as in the Natural, and descending versions of the Melodic Minor scale) or sharped as in the Harmonic Minor and ascending versions of the Melodic Minor scales. Below are the triads generated by these scales.

Ex. 1.27A – Ascending Melodic Minor Scale Chords (Descending is the same as the Natural Minor)

Ex. 1.27B – Harmonic Minor Scale Chords

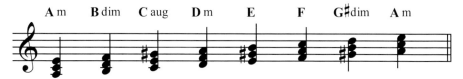

You'll notice a new chord on the third degree of the Harmonic and the Ascending Melodic Minor scales—this is the C Augmented triad. The C Augmented triad is made up of two consecutive Major thirds; it's similar in construction to the diminished triad made of two Minor thirds.

Ex. 1.28

These two chords do not appear in music with anywhere near the frequency of Major, Minor and Dominant seventh chords. It's good to be aware of their existence, but you can play a lot of Blues music without ever encountering them.

This can be a lot to process. Basically be aware that there will be some variation in certain notes in a Minor melody and also in the accompanying chords. On the following page we have three examples of this. Example 1.29 uses the Natural Minor scale. Example 1.30 uses the ascending version of the Melodic Minor scale, and Example 1.31 uses the Harmonic Minor scale. These are all 12 Bar Minor Blues. You'll notice that the chords generated by the Natural Minor scale sound more "Minor-ish" than the others. Next are the Harmonic Minor chords and finally the Ascending Melodic Minor exercise which tends most toward a "Major-ish" sound. I think the most important factor in a Minor key is the Minor third between the root and third. The choices available on the sixth and seventh degrees are more on the level of color options than anything else. The Minor third between the root and third is always the critical difference between a Minor and Major key.

Ex. 1.29 – A Natural Minor Blues

Ex. 1.30 – A Meldodic Minor Blues

Ex. 1.31 – A Harmonic Minor Blues

Let me add one final progression before we leave the Minor keys. This is a Minor Blues using the chords from the Harmonic Minor scale. Instead of the V7 (E) chord in bar 9 going to the iv Minor (Dm) chord in bar 10 (Ex. 1.31), we have the VI major chord (F Major) in bar 9 going to the V7 (E7) chord in bar 10. This is very common in Minor Blues. I use it in "Mike's Revenge" in Chapter 3 (a Minor Blues with the repetition of bars 9 and 10 two extra times).

Ex. 1.32 – A Blues from the Harmonic Minor Scale

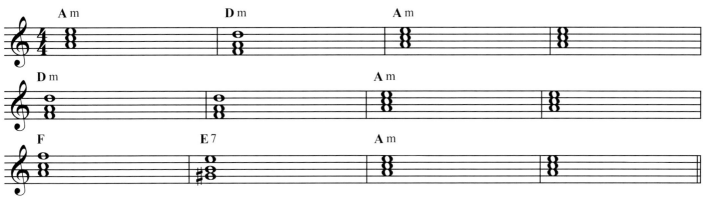

Chapter 2 – **Playing with a Band**

Accompaniment

Webster's Dictionary defines an accompaniment as "something that goes along with another thing: especially music played along with a solo part." *The Harvard Brief Dictionary of Music* calls it "the musical background provided for a principal part." For instance, in piano music, the left hand often plays chords which serve as an accompaniment for the melody played by the right hand. Similarly, a solo singer or instrumentalist may be accompanied by a pianist."

These words expose an underlying truth about music; some things are more important than other things. Listen to any piece of music you really like. You'll notice that at any point in time, some instrument or voice is the primary focus of attention while another (or an entire group) will be in the background supporting it. The spotlight may be on the singer at one point, the lead guitar solo at another, and even the keyboard at another. To play successfully with other musicians, you have to be aware of this fact and know how to alter your playing accordingly.

Let's start with the most basic situation, a pianist's left hand accompanying their right hand. Note that all of the following exercises are played in the swing style (excluding the 12/8 time signature which is as written). Note that most of these examples can be played along with a full-length band track found on the recording for my other book *Blues Keyboard Play-Along Trax* (MB21062BCD).

TRACK
disc 6   **Ex. 2.1 – C Blues**

You'll notice two things about Example 2.1. First, the left hand (the accompaniment) is in a lower register than the right hand. Secondly, the right hand is more active than the left. It acts more like a solo voice; it doesn't just play a repetitive pattern. This is a good illustration of the basic rules of accompanying. The accompaniment should be in a different range (high or low) than the principal part, and it should be pattern based, that is, it should be repetitive to a degree. This helps keep it in the background and provides a non-distracting support for the melody.

Another way of looking at this is: "Melody is King." Regardless if it's a wailing blues vocal, the first violin of a string quartet, or your right hand soloing, there is nothing in good music that overshadows the melody. To be a good accompanist you need to support the melody in an interesting and creative way without distracting from it. And this is what playing in a band is all about.

There's talk these days of the "Zero Sum" game. That is, there is only one winner, and subsequently one (or more) losers. Well, playing music in an ensemble is just the opposite of that. You all win or all lose—together. To someone in the audience, a successful performance will be judged not on the lead guitarist's solo or the drummer's beat, but on how well all the various parts fit together. And to have everything fit together requires that each musician listens to the others and adjusts his playing accordingly. This includes all aspects: timing, tuning, dynamics, note choice, rhythm pattern and texture.

Doubling

There are some musical situations in which the best accompaniment part is already given to you—it's being played by another instrument. This is demonstrated in example 2.2 below.

Ex. 2.2 – Cm Blues

In this tune the bass part is catchy and repetitive. You can double it with your left hand. The right hand part doubles that of the guitar. This works until the V chord later in the tune. At that point you'll switch to block chords, which we'll discuss later. The main point is that somethimes the best part for you to play comes from what others are already playing. Always check to see what they're doing and see if doubling it makes good sense.

Example 2.3 is another example of doubling the bass and taking a part from the guitar. In this piece you can double the bass all the way through. You'll need to get together with the bassist beforehand and decide between yourselves exactly what notes will be used (defer to them if necessary, you're poaching on their turf). As long as neither of you deviate, the groove will be rock solid. In your right hand you'll be playing chords on the off-beat along with the guitar. When the guitarist solos, you just keep playing the chords. This style is called **Jump Swing**. Jump Swing was popularized in the 1940's by artists such as Louis Jordan.

Ex. 2.3 – F Blues

Our last example (Ex. 2.4) of doubling comes from this 8 bar New Orleans style Blues called the Stroll. Here the piano doubles the bass with this loping line characteristic of New Orleans Blues. In the right hand we play various chords and fills to be discussed later, but once again the left hand adds to the groove by doubling the bass.

Ex. 2.4 – The Stroll – F Blues

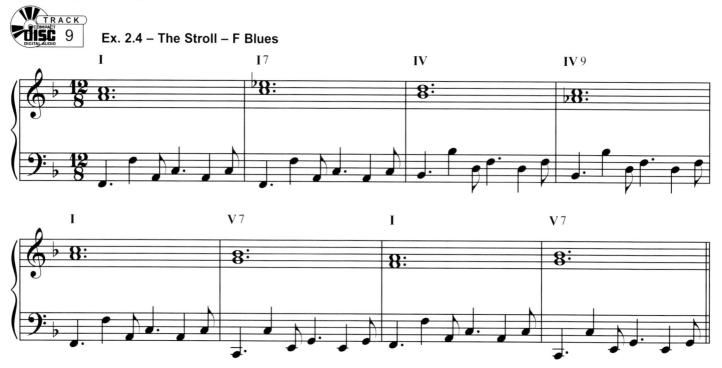

Well, that's pretty much all the low hanging fruit in terms of parts. Most often the piano has to find its own space to fit in the music. But always keep your ears open for an iconic, repetitive bass line or another instrumental part that you may be able to double.

Rhythm Piano

There are a few rhythms that crop up over and over again in the Blues as accompaniment riffs. In swinging blues, medium to up tempo, the **Charleston Rhythm** (Ex. 2.5) can be used to good effect. You play your chords on beat "1" and on the "and" of 2 in each measure. The chord on beat "1" is usually short and the chord on the "and" of 2 will be held to beat four.

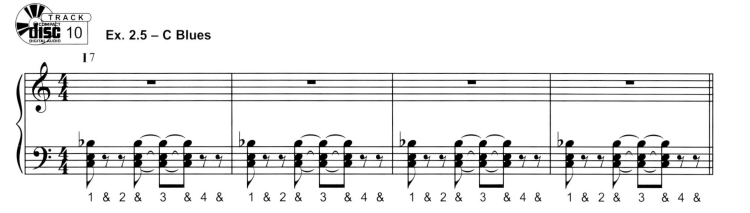

Ex. 2.5 – C Blues

Here's an example at a fast tempo (Ex. 2.6). This is a Swing Blues in B♭ using rootless chords (we'll discuss rootless chords a little bit later). Note that guitar commonly doubles the rhythm with you.

Ex. 2.6 – B♭ Blues

Another example at medium tempo is this organ groove. Note that the organ sounds one octave lower than written.

Ex. 2.7 – G Blues

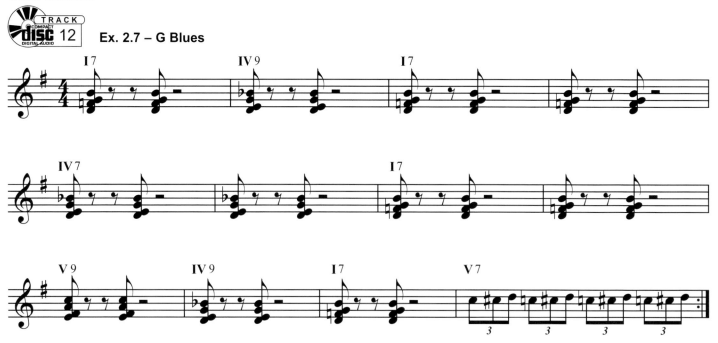

In a Blues with a pronounced 12/8 feel, you can hit chords on every eighth note triplet along with the drummer's hi-hat (Ex. 2.8). Make sure you're well synchronized with the hi-hat. Remember, in general your parts should be completely in synch with any other instrument playing the same rhythm pattern. If you're not doubling that instrument's part, then you should be playing a completely different pattern. Close is only good in horseshoes and hand grenades!

Ex. 2.8 – G Blues

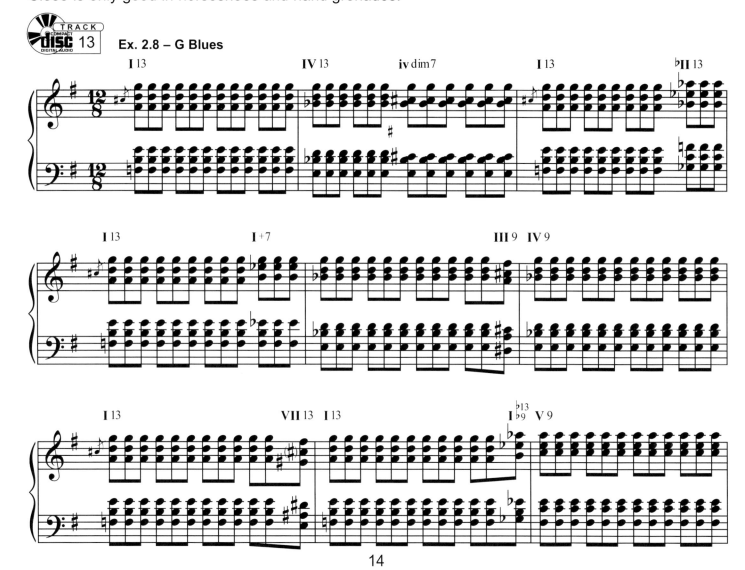

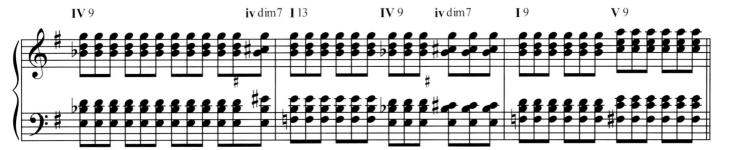

Here's another common rhythm pattern for you to try. Here it's over a **Two-Beat** or **Cut-Shuffle** as I've heard it called.

TRACK disc 14 **Ex. 2.9 – E Blues**

You may deviate from this rhythm from measure 17 (V7 chord) to the end of the chorus by playing sustained chords if you wish, just to break it up.

Side note: All of these song examples (Ex. 2.6 through Ex. 2.9) can be played as full-length songs in my other book and CD within the *School of the Blues Lesson Series*, called *Blues Keyboard Play-Along Trax* (MB21062BCD). Here the keyboard part is muted so that you can practice playing along by yourself.

On the following page (Ex. 2.10) is another characteristic keyboard riff stolen from the guitar. It hits on beat "2" and the "and" of 2 (more specifically the "and" of 2 in a 12/8 feel is the third triplet of the beat—as is the case in all swing eighth feels). It's another pattern particularly suited to the medium tempo 12/8 feel. Note that the organ sounds one octave lower than written.

Ex. 2.10 – G Blues

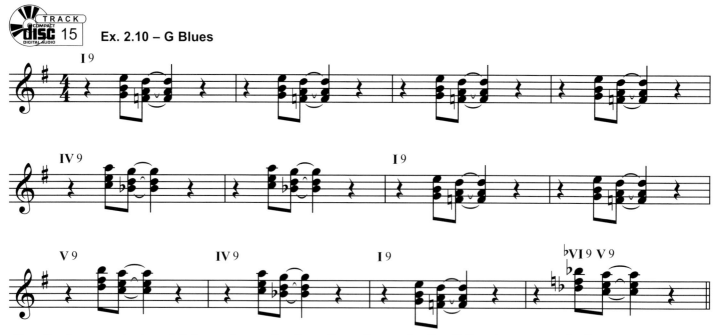

Our final example is a bit less dogmatic than the others. In the following example I've constructed a pattern which anticipates the chord by being played on the "and" of 4 of the preceding measure. I call this **Playing Into The Beat**. I'm actually playing the chord before it's ordinarily played by one half a beat. Some would say I'm anticipating the chord or the chord change. This technique can provide just the impetus a tune needs in certain situations. Use it with some discretion. You'll notice I deviate from it in bars 3 and 4 and return to it in bars 5 and 6.

Ex. 2.11 – G Blues

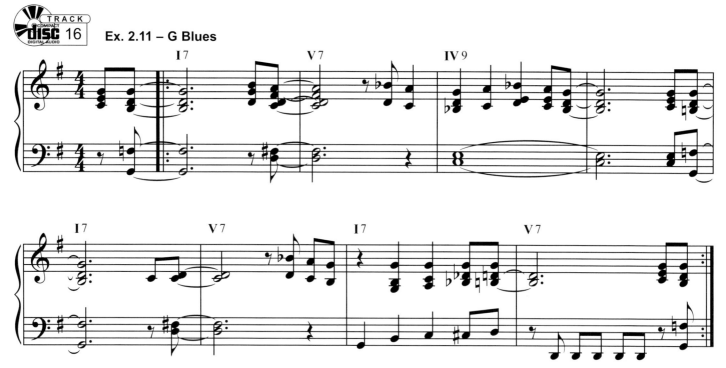

What I'd like you to take away from the preceding section is the following: We're not always the center of attention in life or music, and there are times when it pays to play the background role graciously—learning to be a member of the musical boiler room propelling the great ship of song. You can become a very popular musician by being a good accompanist. Don't worry, you'll get your chance to shine—in a later chapter.

Accompanying Yourself

Here's a question I'm often asked: What do I do with my left hand while I'm soloing? It's a good question, and I have several different answers depending on the situation. As we've shown before, there will be times your left hand will be doubling the bass in a song. You can always keep that bass line going and solo with your right hand. Examples 2.12 and 2.13 demonstrate this.

Now this can all be fairly challenging if you're not one of those keyboardists who are naturally wired to play bass lines (you organ players know who you are!). So, several alternatives are possible here.

In Example 2.13 (previous page), the pianist's left hand is playing the standard dotted quarter note bass figure that he might use when playing solo. If the left hand part is kept out of the deep bass range and the bassist is sticking mostly to roots and fifths, this will work throughout the song. In fact, if you listen to Blues players like Jimmy Yancey who recorded on the acoustic piano with an acoustic bass, you'll hear that the bass and piano double their parts in a very loose way. Because of the tonality of the two instruments, clashes are not that noticeable. For modern players, the situation is different. Electric bass and keyboard allow much less latitude for inaccuracies in the lower register, especially if the bass control on your keyboard is turned up. There's too much sound vying for too little acoustic space. Therefore, I'm going to present you with some options.

Let's look at the chords in a C Blues. We should be able to use them as an accompaniment for our soloing if we choose them wisely. Example 2.14 contains a set of chord voicings in the key of C which will add harmonic support to your right hand work while remaining low enough to not cut up too much of your soloing space on the keyboard. As you can see, these are three-note Dominant 7th chords. Usually the 5th or the root is omitted because the bass will be supplying those and because we don't want a texture that's too thick. This accompaniment uses the Charleston rhythm mentioned before. It may be hard to keep this going while you're involved with your solo, but don't worry, this is your only your accompaniment. It needs to stay out of the way of your fancy runs, so if it drops out, or starts to play the same rhythm as the right hand, that's okay. Also, try to make sure you balance your hands. The left hand part will naturally come out louder because it has three notes (heavier notes too, because they are lower in pitch). Make sure it's not overshadowing your right.

TRACK
disc 19   **Ex. 2.14 – C Blues**

If the voicings above are still too heavy, try these voicings for Example 2.15. Now we're down to "two-note shells" as they're called—there are no roots in these at all.

TRACK CD 20

Ex. 2.15 – C Blues

Here's another shell option. Here we have the Root and the Seventh or the Root and 3rd.

TRACK CD 21

Ex. 2.16 – C Blues

Finally, I'll give you some of the jazzier voicings I like to use. You'll notice the 3rd and 7th from the previous voicings along with the 9th or the 13th of the chord. This gives them a more sophisticated sound.

Ex. 2.17 – C Blues

Remember, here you're trying to do two things at once; solo with your right hand, and accompany with your left. As an accompanist, the left hand must support to the right. It can add a little or a lot, but it can't overshadow the melody.

A side note: When you're not soloing, you can still use these left hand voicings to good effect in the rest of the song. You can double them in the right hand an octave up, or use them to support triads, octaves, or fifths in the right hand. This is demonstrated in Examples 2.18 and 2.19.

Ex. 2.18 – Rootless Shells with Octave and 5th (C Blues)

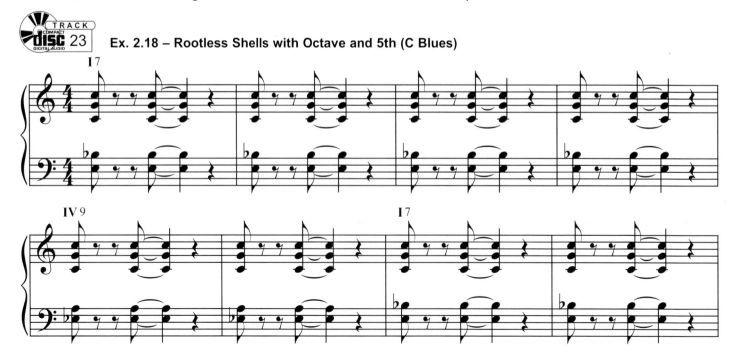

Ex. 2.19 – Root Voicings with Triads on Top (C Blues)

The study of chord voicings is endless. Where you play your voicings is important as well. Here are the ones I gave you before—now in the key of G. This will allow you to play in the keys of F through B♭ without going up too high.

Ex. 2.20 – Chords in G

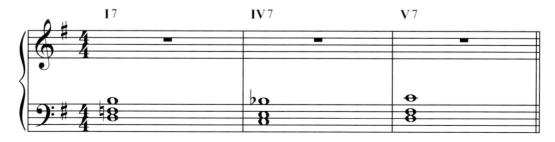

Ex. 2.21 – Chords in G Rootless

Ex. 2.22 – Chords in G Shells

Ex. 2.23 – Chords in G Jazzier

Ex. 2.24 – Chords in G Jazzier with Octaves and Fifths

Ex. 2.25 – Chords in G Shells with Triads

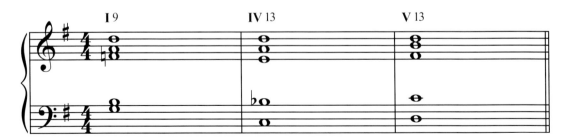

Chapter 3 – **Songs**

In this chapter I'd like to present a couple of tunes that I've written to illustrate different piano techniques. Our first tune is called **"Steve's Blues"** and it's a twelve bar Blues in G without the quick change and with a V-IV-I in the last four bars. There is a two-bar intro, and a similar two-bar turnaround used at the end of the piece. Half of the intro is used in the bar preceding the return of the head in Chorus 6, helping to transition back to the last head.

You'll notice I double up the rhythm of the bass part when we hit the solo section. This gives the arrangement more punch by distinguishing between the heads and the solo. For the solo section, I try to build through the three choruses by starting in the middle register and moving higher as I proceed along. I also try to play a bit more actively as the piece progresses.

Steve's Blues

By Steve Czarnecki

24

25

Our next tune is another composition of mine called **"Mike's Revenge."** I like to call it a Minor Blues with a four bar extension. Up through the 10th bar, it functions as a Minor Blues in C. The repetition of the A♭13, G7sus4 chord changes add the extra four bars for a total of 16.

As you listen to the recording, you'll notice that the piece is in straight-eighths—there is no swing feel here. I still feel it is a Blues despite the change in form and rhythmic feel. As I solo over it for three choruses notice the repetition of the beginning phrase of each 16 bar section. This helps ground the solo as I go through it. I'm actually playing two 8 bar solos in each 16 bar chorus. I keep one theme for the first eight and develop another related one for the second eight. From a harmonic perspective, I use a lot of the C Minor Blues scale here.

Note that you can hear the full version of this song on my CD *Soul Rendezvous, Steve Czarnecki's Soul/Jazz Quintet* (PMP 015) available for purchase on my website www.soul-jazz.com.

Mike's Revenge

By Steve Czarnecki

Chapter 4 – **Musical Material**

Right Hand

In this section I'm going to present some basic musical material you can use in your right hand either with a band or when playing solo. As we discussed before, the left hand will vary when playing with other instruments depending on what they are and whether you're accompanying or soloing. It may be good to refer to the Chorus Forms section in *Blues Keyboard Method, Level 1* (MB 21060BCD), since some of this material can best be understood using the Chorus Form concepts.

Below are a series of short musical phrases, or licks, which capture the sound of the Blues and which you can use to build a Blues solo. Play all of the following examples with a swing feel. Example 4.1 is in the key of C and can be used over the I7 (C7) chord. Since it's only two bars long, you may want to play it twice to cover the first four bars.

  Ex. 4.1

Here's the same lick slightly altered to work over the IV7 (F7) chord.

Ex. 4.3

For the V7 (G7) chord you can use the lick in its original form again (Ex. 4.1). A good bass line under these licks would be this one.

  Ex. 4.3

Here's another simple repeated one bar phrase.

Ex. 4.4

You may use this phrase without alteration over the IV7 (F7) chord if you wish. This sort of harmonic mismatch is often heard in the playing of some of the earlier Blues players. If it bothers you, play it like this.

Ex. 4.5

Over the V7 (G7) chord, use the following phrase; it has the general form of the same lick moved up.

Ex. 4.6

Here's another example of a simple one bar phrase repeated.

Ex. 4.7

For the IV7 chord you may alter it like below or you may leave it the same.

Ex. 4.8

Over the V7 use the original lick again. Example 4.9 is a similar phrase as the ones above.

Ex. 4.9

You can use it over the F7 chord as is or alter it so.

Ex. 4.10

You may notice the similarity in construction in all these phrases. They are influenced by a classic Blues by the great Blues artist Jimmy Yancey called "Yancey's Special." Of course in his recording there are many other elements which come together to make this a great piece of music, but I think the simplicity of the musical ideas and their development provide a good lesson for anyone interested in the essence of Blues piano.

Below are some general Blues phrases in various keys to help you round out your Blues vocabulary.

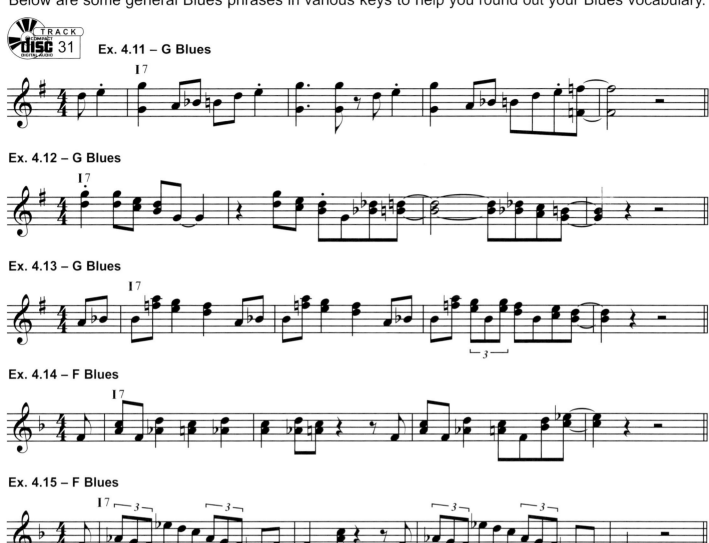

Ex. 4.11 – G Blues

Ex. 4.12 – G Blues

Ex. 4.13 – G Blues

Ex. 4.14 – F Blues

Ex. 4.15 – F Blues

In our study of Chorus Forms from the first book, you'll recall that several of the forms present a different phrase for the last 4 bars (the **C** of an **A B/A C** Chorus Form, for example). I've noticed that many of my favorite Blues performances not only have a strong, but identical C section at the end of each chorus! I feel that a strong **C** section at the end of chorus can salvage a chorus with a less-than-perfect material in its first 8 bars. Therefore, below I've presented some particularly strong **C** sections.

Here is an example similar to the last 4 bars of every chorus in "Yancey's Special."

Ex. 4.16 – C Blues

If that is technically daunting, here's a simpler version.

Ex. 4.17 – C Blues

Below is an example that's similar to the last four bars of "Talkin' Boogie" by Little Brother Montgomery.

Ex. 4.18 – F Blues

That might be a bit challenging. Here's a simplified version.

Ex. 4.19 – F Blues

Finally, here's an example similar to the last four bars of "Mournful Blues" by Jimmy Yancey. It's in the key of B♭ and is played at a slow tempo.

Ex. 4.20 – B♭ Blues

Left Hand

We discussed above the role of the left hand in Blues piano. Basically we can either play chords or double the bass line with the bass player. Here are some more bass lines below. This idiosyncratic part (courtesy of Ray Charles) is probably one you'll never play with a bassist. It's more for solo work. I have provided some tempo markings for you in the following examples. These are general recommendations—play at the tempo that feels right to you.

TRACK 33   **Ex. 4.21 – B♭ Blues**

Here is one slow enough to be doubled with the bass.

TRACK 34 — **Ex. 4.22 – G Blues**

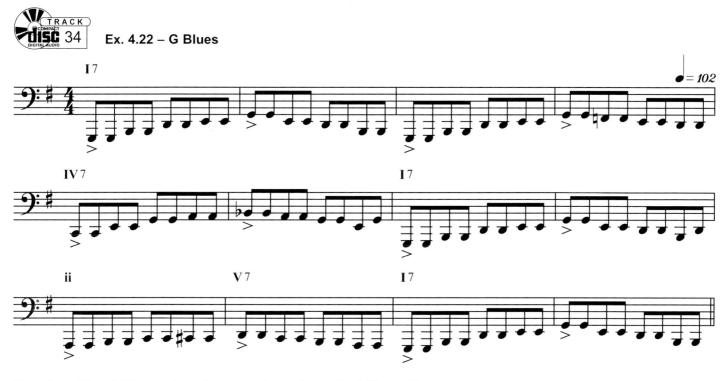

Here's a Floyd Dixon-style line used on piano that fits well.

TRACK 35 — **Ex. 4.23 – G Blues**

The tempo of our next example is faster. We're entering into boogie piano territory. Practice this slowly at first. Eventually you'll get a feel for it and it will be easy.

disc 36 TRACK   Ex. 4.24 – C Blues

We're going to up the tempo for this one, too. I've included the right hand comp (accompanying) pattern for this bass line. Notice that the last four bars come from Ex. 4.18 a few pages back.

disc 37 TRACK   Ex. 4.25 – F Blues

Chapter 5 – **Blues Organ**

In this section on the Hammond organ in Blues, I'd like to spotlight one of the masters of the Hammond, who, while he played Jazz, always claimed to be a Blues player. I'm talking about Jimmy McGriff. With Jimmy McGriff, we hear someone who doesn't play a lot of notes, but does play a lot of music. Below I've taken some characteristic licks from one of his later recordings, *The Starting Five*, and laid them out for you with appropriate bass lines. Jimmy McGriff's upper manual setting is usually something like 888 800 000 with percussion set on soft, fast, third. The bass setting is 838 000 000 (as it is for most players who are playing the bass line on the lower manual).

The first four are in B♭. Play at a medium tempo and note the variety of rhythmic figures.

Ex. 5.1

Ex. 5.2

Ex. 5.3

Ex. 5.4

Here are a few more examples, this time in G.

I can't leave you without something from the most influential jazz organist, Jimmy Smith. His signature sound was: 888 000 000 percussion on, soft, fast, third. Earlier in his career he used Chorus setting three for both manuals and the Leslie set to Stop or Fast. In later years he moved on to no Chorus with the Leslie on Slow or Fast. They both worked equally well, surprisingly enough.

Ex. 5.8

Ex. 5.9

School of the Blues Staff
Front Row (L-R): Frank De Rose, John Garcia and Kevin Coggins
Back Row (L-R): Steve Czarnecki and David Barrett